Painting Flowers on Cakes

Dedication

I dedicate this book to Mark and Zoe. Our Mum
would have been so proud of us. You are my
motivation and inspiration. I am blessed to
have you as my brother and sister.

Painting Flowers on Cakes

Stephanie Weightman

SEARCH PRESS

First published in Great Britain 2013

Search Press Limited
Wellwood, North Farm Road,
Tunbridge Wells, Kent TN2 3DR

ISBN: 978-1-84448-951-0

Suppliers

If you have difficulty in obtaining any of the materials and equipment mentioned in this book, then please visit the Search Press website for details of suppliers: www.searchpress.com

You are also invited to visit the author's websites:

www.cakecrafting.co.uk
www.mycupcakeclub.co.uk

Publisher's note

All the step-by-step photographs in this book feature the author, Stephanie Weightman, demonstrating how to paint on cakes. No models have been used.

Printed in China

CONTENTS

INTRODUCTION

Ever since I learned to paint, I have loved the idea of painting on cakes. Over the years I have tried many different food colouring materials with varying degrees of success and it was only after exhausting almost all edible media that I discovered using edible food varnish and edible powder food colour to make paint. It was like a revelation. I knew that if the consistency and open time of the paint were controllable it would be possible to paint, highlight and shade all in one go, the way I was taught using acrylic paints nearly twenty years ago by the amazing Donna Dewberry.

Many of us grow up believing we are not artistic, however if I were to inquire, most people would concede that they consider themselves creative. This is more than enough for you to become proficient in this style of decorative painting. Before you look at the amazing photography and think, 'I couldn't possibly do that!' I would ask you to remain open-minded and give it a go. I am sure you will be rewarded with some fantastic results.

Take your time to practise the strokes before going on to your finished cakes. I work on acetate when I am trying out a new design and the great thing is, when you have finished, you can hold the result over your cake and imagine what the design will look like when painted directly on to your iced surface. Also, do try varying the size of the flowers and leaves in one design. Simply use a smaller brush for smaller flowers and leaves. Varying the size can really add dimension. With dimension in mind, I sometimes let the colour or pigment run out on my brush by picking up varnish alone, so the colour gets lighter and lighter. The result is a more transparent effect which can be quite striking and provide the finishing touch to a design.

When you have mastered all the different brush strokes and planned your design, choosing colours can be quite daunting. Do not be put off by looking at colours and thinking they may not go together. This is where the little trick of not cleaning your brush between colour changes really helps. Having a hint of the previous colour left on your brush not only helps the colours to tone with each other, but also gives you a natural blending effect which makes it look as though you have spent hours colour mixing. By using just three different colours you can colour shade and highlight in simply dozens of shades. It really is a clever way of painting. The key is always making sure you keep the light and dark colours on separate sides of the brush and always put the light shade on the same side and the dark shade on the opposite side. When you paint, if you find the colours bleeding together and getting 'muddy', you have probably picked up too much varnish on your brush. Clean your brush, dry it thoroughly and start your brush loading again. Once you get started painting, you will find the time just flies by even though many of the designs take minutes rather than hours to finish. This means it will not be long before you are admiring, then eating, your finished works of art.

MATERIALS

There are ever increasing numbers of new materials for cake decorating, however all the cakes in this book can be made then decorated with a small, traditional range of cake tins and readily available tools.

Cake

A square Victoria sandwich, a fruit cake, chocolate cake and cupcakes.

When it comes to decorating cakes, fruit cake is the most traditional style that comes to mind. Fruit cakes are normally quite heavy and dense with a relatively low flour but high fruit content, and this cake stores well.

A basic Victoria sandwich recipe is buttery, spongy and light. It is perfect for large, small or cupcake-sized cakes and can be cut and shaped when cool. This delicate cake can be flavoured with vanilla extract or orange or lemon zest.

Chocolate cake can be light and fluffy or dense and moist and doesn't often last long enough to worry about storage, but it will normally keep well for 4–5 days.

Cake tins come in all shapes and sizes. Some are coated with a non-stick surface and some require you to line the tin or use paper cases; check your recipe for the most suitable method. If you are only going to use a special shaped tin once, consider hiring it from your local cake decorating shop.

A turntable is extremely useful, although not essential, when cake decorating. Choose one that has a tilting feature if possible.

Keep a variety of cupcake cases in your store cupboard, as they can be the finishing touch when it comes to coordinating the cake design with table decorations.

Cake boards are used to present celebration cakes on. The board is normally covered with icing and the edge with ribbon to complement your design.

Circular cutters are used to cut sugarpaste or sugar sheets to shape.

Cake coverings

Sugarpaste icing is a very sweet, edible sugar dough usually made from sugar and glucose and available coloured or white. You can add colouring to the white variety.

Royal icing is a hard, white icing, made from softly beaten egg whites, icing sugar (powdered sugar), and sometimes lemon or lime juice. It is applied to the cake (normally marzipan-covered in advance) while liquid.

Buttercream is a type of icing used inside cakes, as a coating, and as decoration. It is made using butter, icing sugar, vanilla and sometimes milk.

Marzipan is a paste of ground almonds, sugar and egg whites, mostly used to cover cakes before icing. It can be used for modelling, and you can also paint on it.

Icing sugar is a very fine powdered sugar used to make icing, or sprinkled to prevent other items from sticking to work surfaces.

Sugar sheets are very finely rolled icing that is pliable and easy to handle. They should be kept in an airtight bag between uses to prevent them from drying out. Remove the paper backing before use.

Clockwise from top left: icing sugar in a shaker, royal icing, buttercream, marzipan, sugar sheets, sugarpaste in white and colours.

Painting materials

Edible powder food colours can be mixed with edible confectioner's glaze or varnish to create edible paint. These paints can be mixed using the techniques I show in this book, to create an infinite range of shades.

Palettes are perfect for keeping colours separate.

Nylon bristle brushes are the most hygienic for painting on cakes. You will need a variety of sizes for the projects in this book: round brushes in sizes 1, 2, 5, 6 and 9 and flat brushes in 15mm ($\frac{5}{8}$in), 10mm ($\frac{3}{8}$in), 6mm ($\frac{1}{4}$in) and 2mm ($\frac{1}{8}$in).

Food grade alcohol or isopropyl is used to clean brushes and remove edible varnish.

Edible lustre spray can be sprayed on to sugarpaste, sugar sheets, chocolate, buttercream and marzipan to create stunning lustre effects.

Silver edible glitter is used in the Butterflies cake on page 62. There are two kinds of glitter, both are non-toxic, but one needs to be removed from your cake before eating, while the other is fully edible. Please check your glitter pot before applying to your cake.

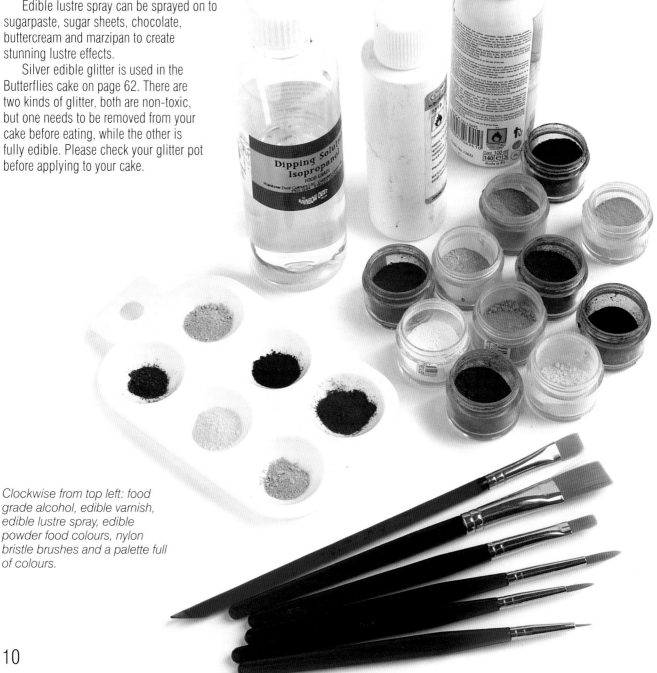

Clockwise from top left: food grade alcohol, edible varnish, edible lustre spray, edible powder food colours, nylon bristle brushes and a palette full of colours.

Other materials

Border punches are a good alternative to decorating with ribbon when used in conjunction with sugar sheets.

Rolling pins come in lots of different sizes. Plastic ones are easy to keep clean and being straight do not leave handle marks on icing.

Smoothers are used for polishing and smoothing icing or marzipan to get a professional finish to the surface. Use like an iron.

Spacers allow you to roll icing or marzipan to an even thickness.

Greaseproof paper protects surfaces and is used to line cake tins, make piping bags and practise brush loading.

Rulers are useful for measuring but also for making straight line impressions.

Palette knives in various sizes are used to lift rolled icing on to cupcakes and cakes and also to smooth royal icing or buttercream.

A pastry brush is used to brush jam or preserves on to cakes.

Various sizes of scissors are useful to cut sugar sheets and baking parchment.

Circle cutters are perfect for cutting circle shapes as toppers on cupcakes and for plaques.

Edible glue is used to stick two icing surfaces together.

Acetate is perfect to practise your design on then hold over the cake to get an idea of size and positioning. Also use acetate to practise brush loading and brush strokes. It feels smooth like painting on icing.

Kitchen paper is used to dry brushes and clean up.

White vegetable fat is used to prevent icing from sticking to your work surface when you roll it out. Smooth a small amount on to the work surface before starting.

Clockwise from top left: border punches, edible glue, kitchen paper, ruler, spacers, greaseproof paper, rolling pins, palette knives, acetate, pastry brush, scissors, white vegetable fat, smoothers, circle cutters.

TECHNIQUES

Cake covering

A covered cake is the perfect surface on which to paint. Choose a cake covering to suit the type of cake and the occasion the cake is being made for. If in doubt, sugarpaste is always popular.

Using sugarpaste

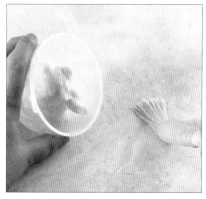

1 Brush white vegetable fat on your work surface to prevent sticking.

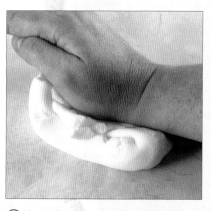

2 Knead the sugarpaste for around three minutes.

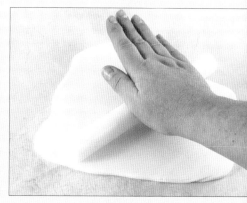

3 Roll it out thinly.

4 Cut out to the correct size using a cutter. This is for a cupcake.

5 Lift the circle of sugarpaste with a palette knife and place it on the cupcake. Smooth the edges with a smoother.

The iced cupcake.

Cutting a sugarpaste plaque

Sugarpaste plaques are quick and easy to make. They are perfect for sponge cakes and can be sized perfectly to fit the top of any cake.

1 Roll out the sugarpaste, put a plate (or other circle of suitable size) on top and cut round it with a sharp knife.

2 Smooth the edges of the circle with a smoother.

3 Slide a palette knife under the circle of sugarpaste and place it on the cake.

The iced cake.

13

Using marzipan and royal icing

Royal icing needs a really smooth surface, and marzipan is not only tasty; it is also ideal on top of a fruit cake to smooth out any little bumps before the royal icing is applied.

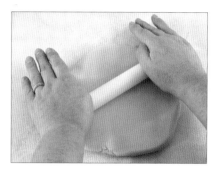

1 Sprinkle icing sugar on your work surface. Knead the marzipan and roll it out to a size large enough to cover the whole cake with some to spare.

2 Brush apricot jam over the fruit cake using a pastry brush.

3 Lift the marzipan on a large rolling pin, supporting it with your hand, and place it over the cake.

4 The cake now has a marzipan 'skirt'. Trim this with a knife.

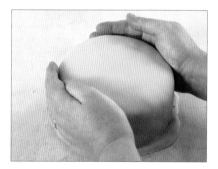

5 Press the marzipan into the cake using your hands and trim it again.

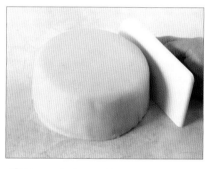

6 Smooth the surface of the marzipan with a smoother.

7 Place greaseproof paper on a turntable and place the cake on top. Spoon the royal icing on top of the cake.

8 Turn the cake and allow the royal icing to run down the sides, helping it into place with a wooden spoon.

10 Wet the palette knife again and continue turning the cake and smoothing the icing. Scrape off the icing that sticks to the palette knife each time you wet it in the hot water.

9 Place a bowl of hot water beside you and wet the palette knife in it. Smooth the royal icing with it, turning the cake as you go.

11 Continue in the same way, smoothing and resmoothing the icing. Towards the end of the process you are aiming to create sharp edges and a neat finish at the bottom.

The iced cake.

Using sugar sheets

Sugar sheets are so useful; they can be painted in advance, stored in a sealed bag and cut out before or after storage.

Making and decorating a plaque

1 Peel the backing off a sugar sheet. Paint a rose on a sugar sheet as shown on page 24. Cover a cupcake in buttercream. Use a cutter to cut out a plaque around the rose.

2 Place the rose plaque on the cupcake.

4 Paint two leaves on sugar sheets, one with one scalloped side (see page 22) and one scalloped (see page 21). Cut out the leaves using scissors.

3 Apply more buttercream in the middle of the first rose.

5 Stick the leaves in the buttercream, then add another rose on top.

The finished cupcake.

Making a border

Decorative borders can be punched from sugar sheets and attached using edible glue.

1 Peel the backing off the sugar sheet and place a strip in a border punch. Punch out the shape, moving along the sheet as you go.

2 Place the border on greaseproof paper and spray it with lustre spray.

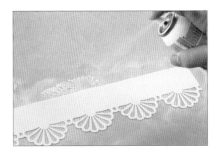

Using chocolate

Chocolate sugarpaste, chocolate cake and melted chocolate are chocolate heaven. For an even more chocolatey version, cover the whole cake in chocolate sugarpaste, pour the melted chocolate over the top and let it run down the sides.

1 Prepare a chocolate cake with buttercream filling and more buttercream around the sides. Knead some chocolate sugarpaste and roll it into a long shape.

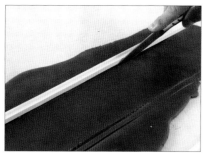

2 Measure the height of your cake. Push cake spacers into the rolled out sugarpaste to create a collar the correct height for the cake. Cut out the collar with a knife.

3 Roll up the collar and offer it up to the cake.

4 Attach the collar to the buttercream round the cake.

5 Cut the two ends with a diagonal cut and join them neatly. Use a smoother to smooth the collar.

6 Melt good cooking chocolate with a high fat content and pour it on the cake.

7 Spread and smooth the chocolate with a spoon.

18

Outlining in chocolate

Chocolate outlines are excellent for covering imperfections, so they might be popular when you first start painting. Try using chocolate in different colours.

A sunflower

1 Paint the sunflower on to a sugar sheet as shown on page 23. Make a small piping bag with greaseproof paper and fill it with melted chocolate. Pipe an outline around the sunflower.

2 Add a highlight in the centre.

A rosebud

1 Paint a rosebud on sugarpaste as shown on page 25. Pipe a leaf outline attached to the stem.

2 Fill in the leaf outline with piped chocolate.

The finished rosebud with a chocolate leaf.

PAINTING TECHNIQUES

A few simple strokes create designs with the wow factor if you use these simple techniques. The most important part of the whole painting process is brush loading. If the brush runs out of paint, make sure it is reloaded perfectly before continuing. If the colours look muddy, you may have used too much liquid, so dry your brush and reload it with colour.

You will need

Palette with green, red, white, black, brown and yellow edible powder food colours and edible varnish

Brushes: 10mm (³/₈in) flat, large round, size 1 round

Sheet of acetate

Turntable and books

Preparing to paint

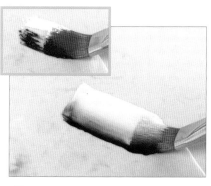

1 Dip a 10mm (³/₈in) flat brush in edible varnish.

2 Dip one corner of the brush in white edible powder food colour, then dip the other corner in green colour so that the brush is double-loaded.

3 Brush on to a sheet of acetate until the grains of powder are crushed into the varnish, making a smooth, workable edible paint in two shades.

A flat leaf brush stroke

1 On your sugar surface, paint a brush stroke, going slightly upwards to start with, then curve down.

2 Flick upwards with the straight edge of the brush to finish the leaf shape.

The finished flat leaf.

A scalloped leaf shape

1 Double-load the brush with green and white as before, crush the grains, then wiggle the brush on the sugar surface to create the scalloped shape.

2 Paint a smooth shape and curve up to finish the first half of the leaf.

3 Complete the lower half of the leaf in the same way, but as a mirror image.

4 Slide the edge of the brush into the leaf to paint a curved stem.

The finished leaf.

A smooth leaf shape

1 Paint a stroke as for the flat leaf shape.

2 Repeat as a mirror image to complete the lower half of the leaf.

3 Add a stem as for the scalloped leaf.

The finished leaf.

Leaf with one scalloped side

1 Paint the top of the leaf as for the scalloped leaf.

2 Paint the bottom half as for a smooth leaf, then add the stem.

The finished leaf.

A poppy leaf

1 Wiggle the brush as for painting a scalloped leaf.

2 Continue the wiggle through several curves, then slide the brush out to a point.

3 Pick up more paint and repeat to paint the other side of the leaf.

4 Slide the brush out to a point.

5 Use the straight edge of the brush to paint a stem.

The finished leaf.

Flat petals brushed together to make a flower

1 Double-load the brush with red and white and paint a flat leaf shape (or in this case, a petal).

2 Paint another petal with the tip finishing at the same point, and continue round in a circle.

The finished flower.

Sunflower

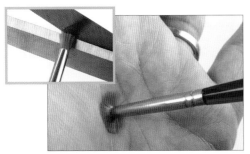

1 Take a cheap round nylon brush and cut across the bristles to customise it for stippling. Crush the bristles to splay them.

2 Pick up black and brown powder food colours and crush them on to the acetate. Paint the centre of the sunflower with the flat, cut part of the brush.

3 Change to the flat brush and double-load it with yellow and white. Stroke on petals, pulling out the dark colour of the centre.

4 Go once round the flower, then reload the brush with yellow and white and go over the petals again to brighten them.

5 Stipple over the edges of the centre to soften them in.

The finished sunflower.

Dots and berries

1 Pick up some varnish on the end of a brush handle and put it on the palette, then mix in red powder food colour.

2 Dot the berries on to the sugar surface using the end of the brush handle.

3 Mix white powder with the varnish in the same way and use a no. 1 round brush to dot on the highlights.

The finished berries.

Rose

1 Double-load the brush with red and white, then paint a petal with a wiggling motion as for a scalloped leaf.

2 Continue round in a circle, adding petals to complete the first layer.

3 Inside the first layer, paint a smooth petal like a flat leaf.

4 Paint the second smooth petal below the first to create the centre of the rose.

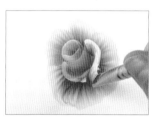

7 Add another smooth petal the other side of the centre.

5 Paint the third smooth petal below this one.

6 Paint a smooth petal at the side of the centre.

The finished rose.

8 Paint a final smooth petal below the centre as shown.

Rosebud

1 Repeat steps 3, 4 and 5 of the rose to create the bud.

2 Leave some colour on the brush and pick up green and white. Paint the first curve of the leaf as shown.

3 Paint a second leaf on the other side, then a third one in front.

4 Paint the top of the stem with a curving stroke below the petal.

The finished rosebud.

Stems and tendrils

1 Use the no. 1 brush double-loaded with green and white. Start with a fairly thick stroke and pull it out, tapering to a point.

2 Continue painting stems from the same point, then change to the no. 10 flat brush and begin to add flat leaves.

The stems with flat leaves.

3 Use the no. 1 brush with green and paint a curling shape, tapering and allowing the colour to fade towards the end. Add several tendrils to the stems and leaves.

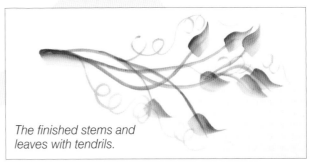

The finished stems and leaves with tendrils.

Bows

1 Use the no. 10 flat brush with red and white and paint two loops as shown.

2 Paint two trailing ribbons from the centre of the bow.

3 Paint a stroke for the centre over the point where the loops meet.

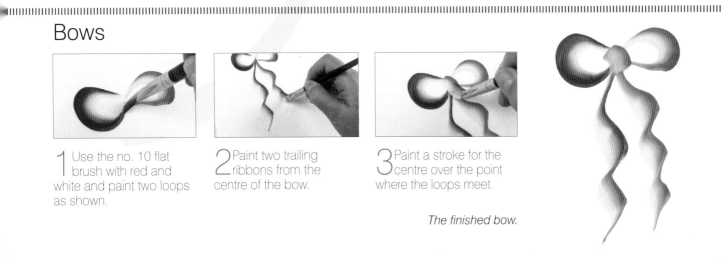

The finished bow.

DAISY CAKE

You can vary the colours of the daisies to suit your colour scheme with this beautiful flower-shaped cake. Decorating the iced cake board by painting with daisies is a lovely finishing touch. Simply use a smaller brush to paint smaller flowers. The daisy designs look great on cupcakes too. Trim the cake with a border punched from sugar sheet using a craft border punch. To ice the board, roll out sugarpaste, dampen the board slightly so the sugarpaste will stick, then roll the sugarpaste on to the board and cut to size. Once you have completed the cake, run double-sided tape round the board and stick the ribbon to this.

You will need

25.4cm (10in) flower-shaped cake and 3 cupcakes, all covered with sugarpaste

30.5cm (12in) iced cake board

Edible powder food colours in primrose yellow, white, orange, brown, citrus green

Edible varnish

Brushes: 6mm (¼in) flat, size 5 round, size 1 round

Yellow ribbon

Sugar sheet, craft border punch and edible glue

1 The daisy design is demonstrated here on a cupcake, but the same one is used on the main cake. Use the 6mm (¼in) brush to paint petals in primrose yellow and white, then paint petals in orange and white over and in between them.

2 Use a size 5 round brush cut for stippling (see page 23) to stipple the centre with brown.

3 Use the 6mm (¼in) flat brush to paint the lines on the petals, using the chisel edge of the brush dipped in orange.

4 Use the size 1 round brush to paint white dots of highlight in the centre. Add flat leaves (see page 20) in citrus green and white.

Right: detail from the finished cakes. The top of the main cake has been decorated with daisies and half-daisies. The iced board is also covered with daisies. The cupcakes have a variety of daisy designs.

TEARDROP CAKES

There are two interlocking Teardrop Cakes, which means that you end up with one to eat and one to keep. Tint white sugarpaste with edible powder food colour to match the flowers. Take a very small amount of edible powder food colour and work it into the sugarpaste by kneading with the heel of your hand. Apply more to darken it until the required colour has been reached. When working with unusual shaped cakes, use thin cake boards and cut them to size using the cake tins as a template. Finish the cake boards with a matching ribbon.

You will need

2 teardrop-shaped cakes, one 20.3cm (8in) and one 25.4cm (10in), covered in tinted sugarpaste

Thin cake boards cut to size

Edible powder food colours in bright blue, navy, green and white

Edible varnish

Brushes: 10mm (³/₈in) flat and 6mm (¼in) flat

Blue ribbon

1 Pick up navy, bright blue and white on the 10mm (³/₈in) flat brush and paint a flower using the technique for a scalloped leaf (see page 21). Paint a bud with the same colours but using flat leaf brush strokes (see page 20).

2 Without cleaning the brush, double-load it with green and white and paint stems, then scalloped leaves as shown.

3 Use a 6mm (¼in) flat brush to paint flat leaves and use more dilute paint to add fainter leaves, creating depth.

Left: details from the finished cakes, shown opposite. The second cake is smaller and nestles next to the first in a yin and yang pattern.

SUMMER ROSES

Roses are the essence of summer and this design makes a perfect party or anniversary cake. Additional cupcakes allow you to indulge yourself in painting when painting one cake simply isn't enough, and they add to the impact of the display. Once the cake has been decorated and put on the board, add double-sided tape around the cake, stick the first, widest ribbon to this, then repeat this process on top of this ribbon, and then again with the narrowest ribbon. Complete by adding the ribbon bows. Trim the board with narrow purple ribbon too.

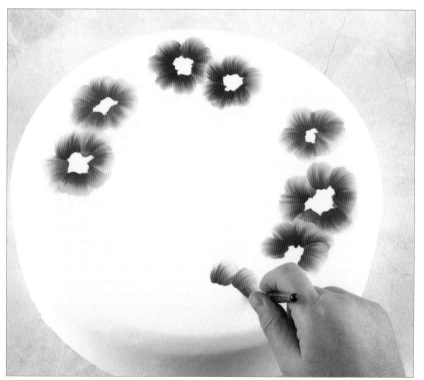

1 Paint the outer petals of the roses as shown on page 24 with mixes of cherry red and white, and burgundy and white. Continue round the cake. Leave two of the roses half completed as shown, as one rose is partly behind another, and one will be partly covered with leaves.

Opposite

The finished cake with cupcakes. One has three roses in autumn shades, using pinks and oranges, with some brown leaves. Another has rosebuds (see page 25) in the same shades as the cake, and the third has a dense pattern of roses in summer shades.

2 Paint the centres of the roses as shown on page 24.

3 Continue adding petals to the roses as shown on page 24.

4 Paint large, dark green scalloped leaves as shown on page 21, then add more in citrus green. Some of the leaves should just go over the edge of the cake as shown.

6 Add smaller flat leaves as shown.

5 Continue adding large scalloped leaves.

Opposite
Detail of the cupcakes.

PANSY CAKE

This pansy design can be adapted for large and small cakes with ease. To get the right colours for the flowers, look at real pansies or find images on the internet and paint them in groups for a full and stunning effect. Once the cake has been decorated and put on the board, add double-sided tape round the cake and stick on the pale green ribbon, then more tape, then the spotted blue ribbon. Above the ribbon, add a decorative border punched out of sugar sheet with a craft border punch. Trim the board with just the spotted blue ribbon.

You will need

20.3cm (8in) cake and 3 cupcakes covered with sugarpaste

25.4cm (10in) iced cake board

Edible powder food colours in bright blue, navy, white, lemon, yellow, dark green

Edible varnish

Brushes: 10mm (³/₈in) flat, 6mm (¼in) flat, size 1 round

Pale green and spotted blue ribbon

Sugar sheet, craft border punch and edible glue

1 Pick up bright blue, navy and white on the 10mm (³/8in) brush and paint the top petals of the main pansies, and the buds.

2 Pick up lemon and navy and paint the green side petals.

3 Without cleaning the brush, pick up yellow and white and paint the lower petals.

4 Paint stems as on page 25 and scalloped leaves as on page 21, using dark green and white. Paint the bracts around the buds using flat leaf brush strokes (see page 20).

5 Use the 6mm (¼in) flat brush to add small green and yellow-green flat leaves to the design.

Opposite

The finished Pansy Cake with cupcakes. These show how you can paint part of the main design – one pansy, two pansies or two buds – to create beautiful cupcakes for any occasion, or to complement your main cake for a big celebration (see detail above).

6 Paint dots in the centres of the pansies with the end of the brush handle and yellow and white, using the technique shown on page 24.

7 Pick up navy and white on the 6mm (¼in) flat brush and touch the pansies close to the centres to create stamens.

Below and opposite

Details from the cake and cupcakes.

8 Dilute dark green with lots of varnish and use a size 1 round brush to paint tendrils, as shown on page 25.

AUTUMN ROSE WEDDING CAKE

If you are looking for a true 'one-off' as a wedding cake, this design definitely fits the bill. The tumbling blue wisteria that complements the roses is perfect for covering up imperfections. The iced board is also painted with the rose and wisteria design for a final flourish. To vary the design, start with large roses on the bottom tier and paint them gradually smaller as you progress up the cake.

Tip

For tiered cakes like this, each cake needs to be on a thick board for stability. You also need three dowels to go through each cake. Push a dowel through into the cake and mark the dowel flat against the top of the cake with a knife, then remove the dowel, trim it to that height and push it back into the cake.

You will need

One 20.3cm (8in), one 25.4cm (10in) and one 30.5cm (12in) cake, all covered with sugarpaste and a board in each size

35.5cm (14in) iced cake board

9 dowels

Edible powder food colours in cherry red, olive green, white, burgundy, orange, citrus green, dark green, blue, soft pink

Edible varnish

Brushes: 10mm (³/₈in) flat, size 5 round, 6mm (¼in) flat

Pale blue ribbon

1 Load the 10mm (³/₈in) brush with cherry red, olive green and white, and paint the stems over the three tiers as shown below.

2 Load one side of the brush with olive green and the other with a mix of burgundy and white. Lay out the leaves (see scalloped leaves, page 21) as the basis for the design with the pink in the centres.

3 Do not clean the brush so that it retains the existing colour, and pick up burgundy and white to begin painting roses. Paint more roses with cherry red and white, and in some, pick up a little orange with the red to create varied autumn shades.

4 Stand back so that you can see any gaps in the design. Without cleaning the brush, pick up olive green on one side and burgundy and white on the other, and add scalloped leaves if required in the gaps. Then add smooth leaves (see page 21), alternating between citrus green and white and dark green and white.

The finished Autumn Rose Wedding Cake on an iced and painted circular board trimmed with blue ribbon.

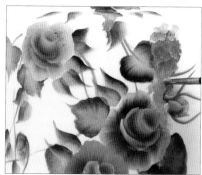

5 Add rosebuds as shown on page 25.

6 Cut a size 5 round brush for stippling (see page 23), pick up blue and white and stipple on wisteria. Vary the shade to build up the three-dimensional effect.

7 Add more white to the mix and paint wisteria cascading down the cake.

8 Double-load the 6mm (¼in) flat brush with soft pink and white, and paint filler flowers with five petals.

9 Paint little flat filler leaves with olive green and a little bit of orange at the edge of the brush to complement the autumn colours. With the colour remaining on the brush plus more varnish, create transparent leaves in the background.

10 Build up all three tiers of the cake with the same elements, with the design cascading down the cake. Paint the iced cake board with the elements of the design, finally adding transparent green and white leaves with the 10mm (³/₈in) flat brush.

11 Paint the front and the back in the same way, then paint a few transparent leaves to link the design as shown.

Right and opposite

Details from the Autumn Rose Wedding Cake.

HEART CAKE

One of the nicest things about this romantic heart cake is that you can use any flowers to join the wicker design and it comes to life when you select flowers in contrasting colours. By overlaying and painting the various elements on top of each other, you achieve a really full effect. I have made mini heart cakes to go with the main cake, and if you made these for an engagement party, anniversary or wedding, you would have something to keep as a memento of the occasion. Trim each cake board with a burgundy ribbon, and add a bow. I have also added a decorative border punched from sugar sheets using a craft border punch.

You will need

One 30.5cm (12in) heart-shaped cake and three 10cm (4in) heart-shaped cakes, all covered with sugarpaste

Thin cake boards cut to size for the small cakes

35.5cm (14in) heart-shaped iced cake board

Edible powder food colours in chocolate brown, white, cherry red, dark green, citrus green, burgundy, soft yellow

Edible varnish

Brushes: 10mm (³/₈in) flat, 6mm (¼in) flat

Burgundy ribbon

Sugar sheet, craft border punch and edible glue

1 Use the 10mm (³/₈in) brush to create the wicker design at the bottom of the heart cake in chocolate brown and white.

2 Paint rosebuds in various sizes (see page 25) to form the top part of the design, using cherry red and white.

3 Without cleaning the brush, pick up yellow and citrus green and put in scalloped leaves. The green will become brighter as you reload the brush and the red clears.

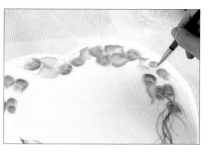

4 Paint in the bracts around the rosebuds (see page 25) and add some flat leaves (see page 20).

5 Pick up cherry red and white and paint a double bow (see page 25) in the centre of the heart.

The finished Heart Cake on a heart-shaped board, trimmed with burgundy ribbon, with three mini cakes. One has a similar design, one has just pink rosebuds and a bow, and one has blue and purple flowers and leaves on one side only.

6 Paint small flat leaves with the 6mm (¼in) flat brush loaded with dark green and white. Build up the design, painting more flat leaves in citrus green and white.

7 Paint blue flowers with five petals in lilac, blue and white with a little burgundy and white. Paint some flowers peeping out from behind leaves, and add tiny round buds lower down.

8 Add browner leaves to the design with chocolate brown with a little burgundy and white.

9 Use the end of the brush handle and a mix of soft yellow and white to dot in the flower centres (see page 24).

Details from the main Heart Cake and a mini cake.

LACE FANCIES

Mini cakes in a variety of colours are a gorgeous tea-time treat, like the French fancies some of us remember from childhood. These lace versions mimic stitched designs with fabric and lace. The sugarpaste is tinted with the same edible powder food colours used for painting (see page 28). Pretty and colourful though they are to look at, these cakes are also delicious to eat and they are easy to paint, too. Place the cakes in cupcake cases for a lovely gift.

You will need

10 cakes 6.3cm (2½in)
square, covered in tinted
sugarpaste
Edible powder food colours
in apricot, white, blue,
green, yellow and pink
Edible varnish
Brushes: 6mm (¼in) flat,
2mm (⅛in) flat, size 1 round

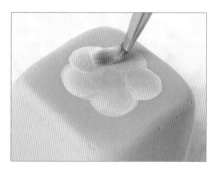

1 This cake is iced with white sugarpaste coloured with apricot edible powder food colour. Take the 6mm (¼in) flat brush, load white on to one side only and paint a faint flower with five petals.

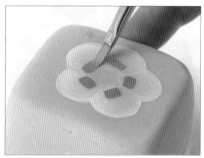

2 Use the 2mm (⅛in) flat loaded with apricot and paint ribbon lines with the flat edge.

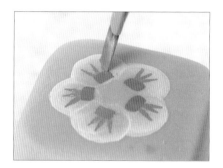

3 Put in the stitches above the ribbons with the edge of the 6mm (¼in) brush and apricot.

4 Use the size 1 round brush with white to paint little dots around the flower. Start going clockwise then alternate and do some going anticlockwise so that the spacing remains even.

5 Hold the cake in a case and use the 6mm (¼in) flat brush loaded on one side only with white to paint a row of curves around the side of the cake. Go round the corners and join up the trim. Complete the trim with upside-down curves underneath.

Opposite

The finished Lace Fancies. In all cases, white sugarpaste was coloured with the same colour edible powder food colour that was used to paint the cakes, so that the colour details are in a stronger shade of the same colour.

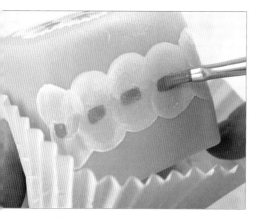

6 Paint apricot ribbons through the middle of the trim as before using the 2mm (1/8in) brush.

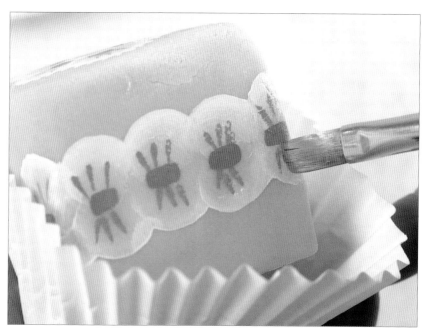

7 Use the 6mm (1/4in) brush to paint sets of three stitches above and below the ribbons with apricot.

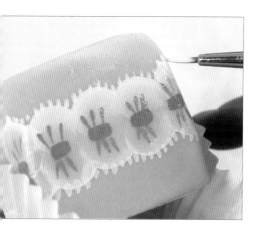

8 Paint little white dots above and below the trim with the size 1 round brush and white.

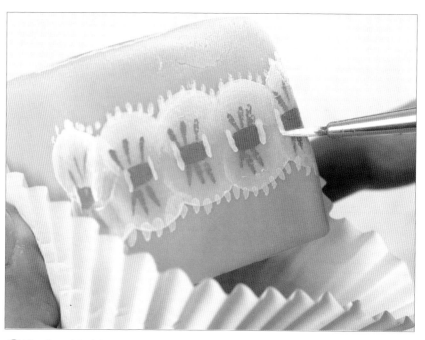

9 Finally add white stitches either side of the ribbons on the trim.

Opposite
A detail of the Lace Fancies.

POPPY CAKE

Poppies are always a favourite, and the bright, vibrant colours against white icing create stunning results. This design is popular with all ages. Finish it off with a decorative border punched out of sugar sheet with a craft border punch, and a flamboyant ribbon with an added bow. To decorate the bow, push in three green leaf hat pins. Trim the cake board with green ribbon.

You will need

25.4cm (10in) oval cake covered with sugarpaste

25.4cm (10in) square iced cake board

Edible powder food colours in cherry red, burgundy, dark green, citrus green, black

Edible varnish

Brushes: 10mm (³/₈in) flat, size 5 round brush, 6mm (¼in) flat

Red and green ribbon

3 green leaf hat pins

Sugar sheet, craft border punch and edible glue

1 Paint the top petals of the main poppy flowers as you would a scalloped leaf (see page 21), with the 10mm (³/₈in) brush loaded with cherry red and burgundy. The darker burgundy should go towards the centres.

2 Paint the side and lower petals in the same way.

3 Paint the buds with little flat leaf shapes, with the burgundy at the top.

4 Without cleaning the brush, pick up dark green and white and paint the main stems (see page 25). Again, without cleaning the brush, use citrus green and white to paint the stems to the buds.

Opposite
The finished Poppy Cake on a square iced board edged with a green ribbon. The ribbon and bow add a final flourish.

5 Paint poppy leaves with dark green and citrus green, following the instructions on page 22.

6 Complete the second side of the poppy leaf.

7 Use a size 5 round brush cut for stippling (see page 23) to stipple the black poppy centres in the main flowers.

8 Pick up dry grains of yellow edible powder food colour and stipple them on to create pollen in the poppy centres. Add small filler leaves in dark green and white with the 6mm (¼in) flat brush.

Opposite
Detail from the Poppy Cake.

EASTER LILIES

This painting technique works just as well on chocolate, as shown in this Easter treat, and of course chocolate is popular at any time of year. Make sure the chocolate is properly set before painting on it; I always put my cake in the fridge for half an hour before I start. Trim the board with a silver ribbon, then a brown one on top.

You will need

30.5cm (12in) chocolate cake with collar and topping as on page 18
30.5cm (12in) cake board
Edible powder food colours in soft yellow, white, burgundy, orange, dark green, citrus green
Edible varnish
Brushes: 10mm (³/₈in) flat, 6mm (¼in) flat
Silver and brown ribbon

1 Double-load a 10mm (³/₈in) brush with soft yellow and white and paint lily petals as shown.

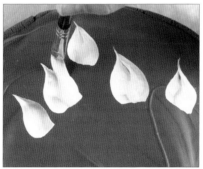

2 Pick up a tiny bit of burgundy over the yellow, and white as before, and paint the second sides of the lilies.

3 Use the 6mm (¼in) flat brush to paint the styles with yellow and orange.

4 Load the brush with dark green and white and paint a stroke at the base of a lily.

5 Paint a second and a third stroke, all leading to the same point, below the flower.

Opposite
The finished Easter Lilies cake.

54

6 Paint the stems (see page 25) with dark green and white.

7 Use the 10mm (³/₈in) brush with dark green and citrus green to paint the lily leaves.

8 To paint the bent back leaf, stop halfway, lift the brush and then sweep it downwards to paint the bent over part.

9 Paint grass with dark green and citrus green, to help tidy up the bottoms of the stems.

Opposite

Detail from the finished Easter Lilies cake.

DRAGONFLY CAKE

This is one of my favourite designs which works really well for a wedding or big celebration. It requires dowels and boards for stability like all tiered cakes (see the Tip on page 38). Whether you paint just one or a number of dragonflies, the design looks stunning and the bottom tier, which is painted all over with flowers, gives the illusion of a delicately printed fabric rather than simple icing. Trim the base of the top cake with a narrow turquoise ribbon, and the base of the bottom cake with a wider one. Cupcakes look great with a single dragonfly design.

You will need

One 20.3cm (8in) cake, one 25.4cm (10in) cake and two cupcakes, all covered with sugarpaste

A cake board in each size

Dowels

Edible powder food colours in kingfisher blue, white, dark green, lilac blue, olive green

Edible varnish

Brushes: 10mm (³/₈in) flat, 6mm (¼in) flat

Wide and narrow turquoise ribbon

1 I demonstrate the dragonfly on a cupcake but it is the same for the main cake. Double-load the 10mm (³/₈in) flat brush with kingfisher blue and white and paint two wings, point to point, as you would petals.

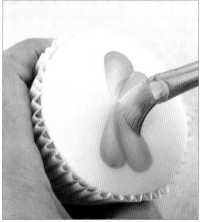

2 Paint two more wings below the first two in the same way.

3 Pick up kingfisher blue, white and a little dark green on the right, on a 6mm (¼in) brush. Stroke down to create the head, in the centre above the wings, then lift the brush off.

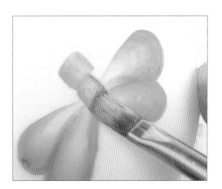

4 Paint the next body section in the same way, directly below.

5 Continue painting shorter body sections, leaving little gaps between them.

Opposite
The finished Dragonfly Cake trimmed with turquoise ribbon, with two cupcakes in kingfisher blue and lilac blue.

6 Curve the body round to the left and make smaller marks for the tail. The dragonfly should go in the centre of the main cake.

7 Pick up kingfisher blue, lilac blue and white on the 10mm (³⁄₈in) brush and paint flowers around the top of the main cake, with five petals as shown. Paint three petals of a flower showing from behind a whole flower.

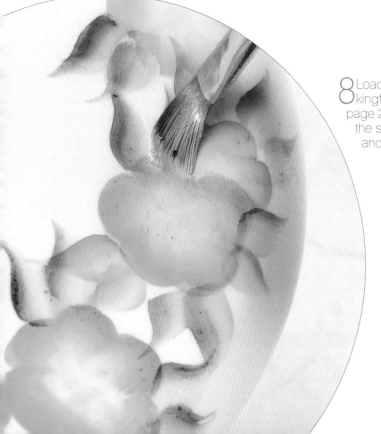

8 Load the brush with olive green, white and kingfisher blue and paint little flat leaves (see page 20). Overlap the leaves in places. Cover the sides of the bottom cake with flowers and leaves in the same way.

Opposite
*Detail of the Dragonfly Cake
and cupcakes.*

BUTTERFLIES

This tiered cake needs dowels and cake boards for stability (see the Tip on page 38). The painted decorations are all the more impressive for being three-dimensional. Simply scattered all over the cake and then dusted with edible glitter, this kaleidoscope of butterflies looks truly magical. Paint dainty leaves and stems as a guide for positioning the butterflies and to peek out as foliage for them to rest on. Trim the bottom cake board with pink ribbon.

1 Paint butterflies on sugar sheets. Use the 10mm (³⁄₈in) flat brush to pick up pink and white and pink with a tiny bit of orange. Paint a petal shape for an upper wing.

2 Wiggle the brush as you would to create a scalloped edge.

3 Paint the lower wing in the same way.

4 Paint the other side of the butterfly in the same way. Make sure the body is deep enough or the butterfly will be inclined to break once it is cut out.

5 Cover a sugar sheet with the butterflies in varying shades of pink, burgundy, orange and soft yellow with white. Cut them out with scissors.

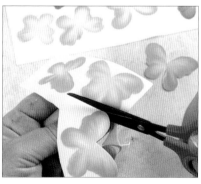

Opposite
The finished Butterfly Cake.

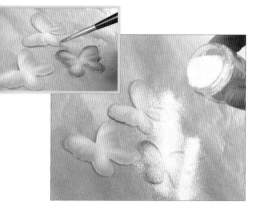

6 Place the butterflies on baking parchment. Use a size 2 round brush to brush edible glue around the edges and tip edible glitter over them. Tip the excess back into the pot.

7 Bend back the butterflies' wings a little and leave them on some dimpled foam so that they dry in this position and take on the realistic shape.

8 Pick up lots of varnish on the 6mm (¼in) flat brush to ensure a transparent paint effect, then pick up dark green and white and paint stems (see page 25) and flat leaves (see page 20) on one corner of a cake and over the edge.

9 Use a transparent burgundy mix to paint flat leaves, then paint some flat butterflies in the same shades as before.

10 Stick the 3D decoupage butterflies over the painted area of the cake using edible glue. Where necessary, you can stick them into the sugarpaste with a pin until the glue dries, then repair pin holes with a very small amount of sugarpaste mixed with water and applied with a brush.

11 Paint and decorate one corner of each cake as shown, creating a cloud of 3D butterflies.

Opposite
Detail of the Butterflies cake.

LAVENDER CUPCAKES

If you have never tried painting before, these quick and easy cupcakes would be a good place to start. Simple stems of lavender crisscrossing over each other to form tiny bunches are the essence of the design. You could even use real lavender to flavour the cupcakes. Tint the sugarpaste with edible powder food colours, using the mix described in step 2, and varying the strength between cupcakes.

You will need

Five cupcakes covered with sugarpaste tinted with lilac edible powder food colours in various strengths (see page 28)

Edible powder food colours in citrus green, white, navy blue, cherry red, lilac blue

Edible varnish

Brushes: 6mm (¼in) flat

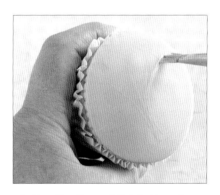

1 Use the 6mm (¼in) flat brush with citrus green and white to paint stems on the sugarpaste plaque on top of the cupcake.

2 To make an edible lilac paint, mix navy blue, cherry red and lilac blue with white. Mix this to a shade darker than your sugarpaste plaque and use the tip of the brush to print little lavender flower shapes.

3 Build up the pattern of the lavender, working your way down the outside edges of the stems.

Opposite

The finished cupcakes. These beautiful cupcakes would make a beautiful spread at a summer wedding or party. Vary the tones of the purples and greens.

4 Reload the brush and paint more lavender flowers down the middles of the stems.

5 Paint more little flowers at the bottom over the stems.

6 Go back and paint more citrus green and white foliage below the flowers.

Details of the Lavender Cupcakes.

SUNFLOWER CAKE

When a large celebration cake is called for, why not make a grand statement with this giant sunflower design? The size of the flower head can be adjusted to fit any size of cake from cupcake to extra large rounds. Trim the base of the cake and board with a wide yellow ribbon and add a brown one on top.

You will need

- 35.5cm (14in) cake covered in sugarpaste
- 35.5cm (14in) cake board
- Edible powder food colours in chocolate brown, white, soft yellow, bright yellow, burgundy
- Edible varnish
- Food grade alcohol
- Brushes: 15mm (⁵⁄₈in) flat, size 9 round
- Wide yellow and narrow brown ribbons

1 Use the 15mm (⁵⁄₈in) flat brush to paint a large circle for the centre of the sunflower in chocolate brown in the middle of the cake. Use large, sweeping strokes.

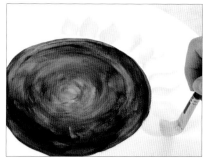

2 Double-load the brush with soft yellow and white and paint petals around the centre, without touching the brown.

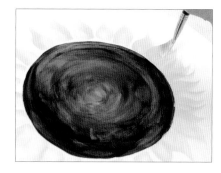

3 Double-load with bright yellow and white and paint more petals in between the first ones.

4 Make sure you paint with random strokes, rather than going round in a circle from beginning to end, or you will end up with a 'windmill effect'.

5 Double-load with yellow and white and a little burgundy so that some petals have a darker edge.

Opposite
The finished sunflower cake. This is perfect for a summer occasion or for someone who loves their garden. The iced board is edged with a yellow and a brown ribbon.

6 Paint edible varnish over the sunflower centre.

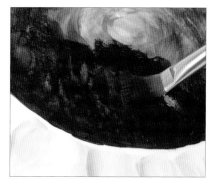

7 Brush in more chocolate brown edible food colour powder while the varnish is wet, to create a textured effect. Pat the surface with a brush to make puddles of paint.

8 While the centre is wet, pull out some of the colour to shade the central parts of the petals.

9 Cut across a size 9 round brush to create a stippling brush (see page 23) and use it to stipple round the edge of the centre, softening its edges.

10 Pick up a little bright yellow on the stippling brush and stipple part of the centre to create highlights.

11 Create a couple of accents in the centre with two sweeps of the stippling brush and bright yellow with white.

12 Pick up a mix of edible varnish, chocolate brown and food grade alcohol and flick the bristles to spatter the mix over the cake.

Opposite
Detail of the Sunflower Cake.

BLACK AND WHITE WEDDING CAKE

This design looks elegant and sophisticated in black and white and would also work well in any colour combinations. Its versatility makes it suitable for almost any occasion or celebration. Trim the top tier with black ribbon at the base, and the two lower tiers with the same ribbon at top and bottom.

Tip

Each cake stands on a thick board for stability, and should have three dowels pushed through it as described on page 38. The tiers are layered using acrylic resin cake stands.

You will need

One 20.3cm (8in) square cake, one 25.4cm (10in) square cake and one 30.5cm (12in) square cake, all covered with sugarpaste

A thick square cake board in each size

Nine dowels

Two acrylic resin cake stands

Edible powder food colour in black and white

Edible varnish

Brushes: 10mm (³/₈in) flat, size 5 round

Turntable

Black ribbon

1 Make sure you have the turntable raised up so that you are working at your eye level. Double-load the 10mm (³/₈in) flat brush with black and white and paint three flat leaf brush strokes (see page 20) along the side of the smallest cake. Paint all four sides in the same way.

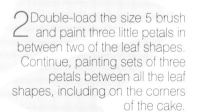

2 Double-load the size 5 brush and paint three little petals in between two of the leaf shapes. Continue, painting sets of three petals between all the leaf shapes, including on the corners of the cake.

74

This stylish, modern cake would bring an understated elegance to a civil ceremony or wedding.

3 Use the end of the brush handle to paint a dot beneath each set of three petals (see page 24).

4 Begin painting the top of the cake with the 10mm (³/₈in) flat brush double-loaded with black and white. Paint a leaf shape.

5 Paint a second leaf shape next to this as shown.

6 Paint the other half of the leaf as a mirror image of the first, as shown. The point of the leaf should point to the corner of the cake. Paint leaves in all four corners in this way. Paint a flat leaf brush stroke (as in step 1) between each leaf, in the centre of each side of the cake top.

7 Change to the size 5 round brush and paint three petals at the top of each leaf as shown.

8 Use the end of the brush to add dots to decorate the petals as shown, (see page 24). This completes the top tier. The middle and bottom tiers are variations on this.

These pages: details from the Black and White Wedding Cake.

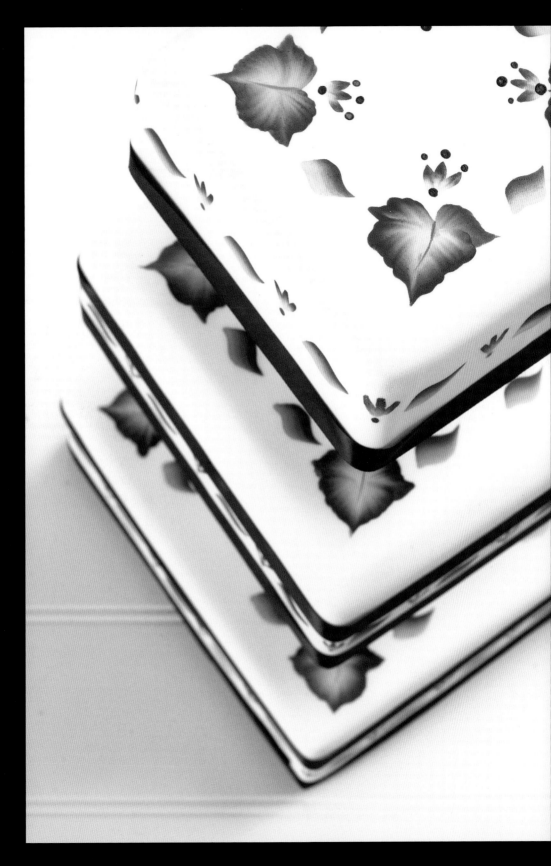

INDEX